EXHALING HELIUM

Victoria Cocolaras

edited by joshua callahan
and dylan cahir

Copyright © 2019 by Victoria Cocolaras

All rights reserved. This book or any portion thereof
may not be reproduced or used in any manner whatsoever
without the express written permission of the publisher
except for the use of brief quotations in a book review.

Printed in the United States of America

First Printing, 2019

ISBN-13: 978-0-578-57922-1
ISBN-10: 0-578-57922-1

To the people and events that inspired these words:
your influence and memory are part of me always
and, now, part of us
is here.

CONTENTS

Soliloquy on Thermodynamics   3

A Pleasure to Burn   6

A Vineyard in Pyrgos   8

Ode to an Affable Stranger   9

Doppelgänger   11

Lips of a Nike Woman   12

To the Artist Whose Painting Hangs in My Living Room   13

In a Field of Sunlight   15

From Your Window, I Can See the World   16

Origami   18

Kissing with Pop Rocks   19

Letter to a World War II Veteran   21

You're beautiful   23

By Request   25

Galileo   26

Descent   28

Questions for the Stranger in Front of the Playhouse   31

Sunset Over Sutphin Boulevard   32

3 a.m. to Coney Island   34

Saunter at the MoMa   35

Chaos Theory   38

Lying Backwards in Bed   40

To Friendship   41

on the steps of one's home   43

The Seconds Between   45

Roadside Memorial   47

purple and orange   49

Galaxy Surfing on a Knitting Needle   51

Call Me Space Cadet   53

evening rhythms   56

Crescendo   58

Bookmark   60

Trees Discovered Sunspots (and We Will Too) *61*

NOTES *65*

ACKNOWLEDGMENTS *67*

May these words inspire you to exhale any helium of your own!
♡ Victoria Cockave

EXHALING HELIUM

May these words inspire you to create and believe in your own!

♡ Aylani Lanae

Soliloquy on Thermodynamics

Let me go down like the sun
over the savanna:
blazing orange, illuminating
silhouettes
of lions, zebras, giraffes, elephants.

Let me roam with them,
be with them,
be *like* them
and tomorrow,
whether or not I come back
in the morning,
let   me   be
thoughts, flesh, [wo]man, animal,
Woman and Animal, Tree,
Leaf, Sprout[ing up
from earth],
aligned in a single harmony
of one, of *om*, of being, energy
(never created nor destroyed,)
one thunderclap, lightning bolt,
tree falling in the distance;

but, let them hear me
when I am not around,
blazing orange, voice of many

from one, force for others, among others,
neither created nor destroyed--
creative, not destroyed

because we are more than we are
when we are born
and less than we are now,
aligned with the rising of the sun;
the way the dark fades
into brighter blue for morning walks
and thoughts to bloom like succulents,
planted like us, our feet
buried in earthen flesh;

the way the sun sets
the sky on fire, sets into
a summer night.

Let me set the world on fire,
be on fire
amidst lions, and succulents,
you, me
(all and nothing)
created to be destroyed.

Let that not be what we come to;
rather, let the flames of your sun
blacken silhouettes to ashes
that rise with phoenixes

and ourselves,

plucked from the same plant,

emblazoned

by the raging orange

that sets

above

the plain.

A Pleasure to Burn

"We come from stardust,"
she told me, hair like spark plugs
and lit fuses, frayed
conductors of electricity verging on combustion,
still ashen
from the last verse
in her book.

She ignited words for a living,
set them ablaze in midair,
held up by their own anti-gravity

(she called it *soul*
us, *source,*
each of our own current.)

I never did set fire to the darkness
nor detonate any souls I know of
but, once,
I saw embers
flicker onto pavement,
the lucid shimmer of Polaris
guiding my words along wire
after wire
as I sat against a backdrop
of evening sky:
starless,
ashen,

verging on combustion.

A Vineyard in Pyrgos

I sit in placid silence beside
a stranger of two weeks, focus
towards drawn curtains, sun

rising over waters I know
but couldn't point to on a map. You stir
in a seat across the aisle, blue

and white collar peeking out
beneath a sweater of burgundy
like the endless spaces between

your yellowed teeth. Youngest
of brothers, oldest of men, smile
of Polaris, but Mount Olympus

is not in Olympia and not all
daughters have fathers but you
look like someone I know

resting at Zeus' temple--vineyards
of Mercouri, navel of earth,
eyes of orange marmalade.

Ode to an Affable Stranger

I. City rush
    shoulder brush
    souls made of the same something.

II. Like dissolves
    like, a same
    something,
    dissolves...

III. Breeze trails through a broken screen
    screw you, screw me
    always *bigger problems out there*:
    me chasing you chasing them

IV. It's *us* you're saving *them*,
    those people--we are not
    strangers.

V. *Chase*
    something.

VI. The Japanese poets
    were right:
    everything is finite.

VII. *No one saves us but ourselves*
    Run to the river
    away from the stream

VIII.   run chase
      them come back
      chase
      you stop I
      stopped staggered
      dizzy
      with inertia

IX.   Breeze trails through a broken screen
      (you look smaller over there)

X.   Familiar, I think
      I passed you on the street once,
      always me (you) them

Doppelgänger

They say
it's both of us
moving,
me with the Earth,
you on your own;

yet, as I watch
your speckled nightcap
bobbing alongside the glass,
through the shadows,
I know I am still.

Lips of a Nike Woman

I see you watching me
with the same interest I watch you,
lioness eyes eroded
by science fairs, paychecks,
futures of men.

Your nose, once lateral
is shaved on one side,
your wings broken by years of flying...
(please leave me to my ignorance.)

Beside you, your sister rests,
austere eyes forever protecting
the secrets sealed behind
your thinning lips.

I lean into the quiet inhales
of your plexiglass home, to find
terracotta missing from your fall off the roof
of that temple in Poros,

your bottom lip split,
secrets like waves flowing
in between the stillness
of our breaths.

To the Artist Whose Painting Hangs in My Living Room

Is that the water
           of the island
                      where you honeymooned?

How can there be shadows
                                        without any light?

           Did you spend years
                in notebook margins
                      working on that signature?

What did your wife say
                          when you chose the watercolors?

Was it the buildings
or people
                that grew stale?

                                          Was it you?

How is it that the yellow   and green
rectangles   seem to be smiling?

What made you

                      silent

                                      that afternoon

              you found those sculptures

                  in her closet?

Whose name   drips   from the edge
                    of your brush?

Why didn't you fix those rusty hinges

                      on that swing

                            in your backyard?

Can fingers

                            forget?

Whose poem pierced your skin

                            as you claimed the canvas?

How does it feel

                  to be

                                  the subject?

In a Field of Sunlight

I was three years old
the first time I watched sunlight
strike my fingers, running
through your hair, wild
like my wishes.

With every breath of the wind
our perfumes fused:
earth
and chocolate milk.

Now, neither sunlight
nor wishes can melt
the frost which so tightly
grips
stuffed elephants,
grandparents,
wristwatches.

Years are erased
but I still watch you, alone
in that field, shivering
beneath the sunlight, faded
like those wishes.

From Your Window, I Can See the World

It looks like turquoise suitcases and vagabond knapsacks,
the picture inside my passport

like amber waves of hair,
parted to the right.

It looks like palm trees
walking into dusk,

like the bottom of a pickle jar
and handguns,

like midnight drives, raccoon eyes,
saltwater pillows

and handkerchiefs,
tied to the end of sticks.

From my window, I can see yours.
It looks like a telephone of string

and empty peanut cans
(I've measured it too.)

On moonless nights,
your desktop reflects

onto the glass
and there's a stillness

where my heart
should beat

with the glow
of Polaris.

Origami

Eyes
squinting in sunlight:
single folds
of the same
sheet
of paper.

Kissing with Pop Rocks

Do you remember
when we walked around
the candy store
in the back of that Cajun shop
off some exit
on the road
in Louisiana?

We shuffled through
rows and jars
of colored confections,
the kinds that made
our parents
who they were
(and us in their image,)
recalling the first time
we ever tasted
the sweets.

You asked me
if I ever kissed
with Pop Rocks.

Where I grew up,
kids did other things
with explosive candies.

Not me, though.

I never even kissed with them.

We walked on
past saltwater taffy
and alligator souvenirs
to the front of the shop,
making our way
for an older woman
coming up the stairs,
left hand clasping the railing
for support,
and an older man
that followed.

I bet they were there
for the Pop Rocks.

As we neared the car,
you slowed your step,
kissed my cheek,
and I felt a tingle
against my tongue.

Letter to a World War II Veteran

I never knew how
to begin letters
when I used to write to you.
I usually ended up
asking about something silly,
like the weather.

It rained here last night.
A thunderstorm, really.
It's always the weather.

It was beautiful, though,
in the way that broken things
are beautiful.
(I think you would have enjoyed it once.)

I wonder a lot
about the things you knew.
(You never told me any of it.)
You might have tried to tell me;
I might have tried to listen.

I remember that story I wrote years back,
about the little boy
who left his home
and family
for something more.

You liked my writing.
You were proud of me once.
I don't think you'd be proud anymore.
The rain was just so heavy.

It's always the weather.

I saw the letter you wrote
when you were my age.
(I don't remember what it said.)
I wonder
if we have
the same handwriting.

You're beautiful
(after Simon Armitage)

because of the way your mouth and eyes work together when you smile.

I'm ugly because my left eye never stays open in pictures.

You're beautiful because the questions you ask don't have answers.

I'm ugly because you can hear the hyphens and semicolons when I speak.

You're beautiful because you gather meaning from *The Catcher in the Rye.*

I'm ugly because I wore Holden Caulfield's hat for trick-or-treating last Halloween.

Ugly is a handgun,

Beauty lives in lore.

Beauty is the tip of tongues,

Ugly makes me sore.

Ugly comes to fill my lungs as

Beauty swims ashore.

You're beautiful because you go to baseball games and share popcorn every time.

I'm ugly because I bought a Jeter jersey the last time the Yankees won the series.

You're beautiful because you place empty bottles on your windowsill for memory.

I'm ugly because I traded my first doll for four dollars at a yard sale.

You're beautiful because your words assert themselves.

I'm ugly because I exhale helium in social circles.

Ugly is a handgun,
Beauty lives in lore.
Beauty is the tip of tongues,
Ugly makes me sore.
Ugly comes to fill my lungs as
Beauty swims ashore.

You're beautiful because you went to school twenty-five hundred miles away from home.

I'm ugly because I used to watch my band teacher order garlic bread from the corner pizzeria.

You're beautiful because your mother lives in Singapore and you visit her every summer.

I'm ugly because I told my father I wouldn't pay for his life support.

You're beautiful because you find substance in my words.

I'm ugly because I find substance in my words.

Ugly is a handgun,
Beauty lives in lore.
Beauty is the tip of tongues,
Ugly makes me sore.
Ugly comes to fill my lungs as
Beauty swims ashore.

By Request

Please
never
trace
my name
with your pen,
for ink is precious

and I fear
to read it
would leave mine
spilling
out
the jar.

Galileo

I first heard about you
in stories read to me,
saw you for the first time
painted by some artist, somewhere
(I remember the brush strokes
in your mustache)
and I recall the first time
I discovered you were a *man of the stars*
and I, being a girl of the stars,
took to you.

You, always looking for something.
You, with your telescope
because you needed to see more
and you found it
through the same lens I've spent
years looking into.

Years pass, all is magnified
and my chest has grown too small
for the heart that's seen Neptune
and the moons of Jupiter.

I am *cardio*centric, a fixed observer.
My telescope's magnified
all that's seen through it
and I am unable to recoil.

I have grown,
become a woman
of the changing tides,
daughter of the moon--
you feel distant;
yet, I stare into vast space
and the darkness begins to pigment
like the various colors
in a brush's stroke.

Your face appears,
shoulders, forearms, fingertips
holding a telescope.
I stretch out my hand
and push it back, I,
constant observer,
cardiocentric,
girl of the stars.

Descent

...the brain sends out a signal that it's dying...the body receives it, and after a while, the body thinks it's dying too...

Lately, everything tastes like cherry coffee
after a burnt-tongued
first sip--back to the matter
at hand.

You told me I argue too much
so somewhere down the line,
I stopped reading
between them,
stopped reading,
stopped eating meat.
(You told me about the acid trip
that made it all lucid, the way
of the world,
a lotus, before you.)

I took it further (I often do,)
refused to let my lips
touch anything
brutality touched,
except for you.
(I didn't know it at the time.)

You said my lipstick remains
a stain
on your thoughts, please,
keep it there for memory.

You thought I was like you,
in that boxed wine way,
that turns an iris
to slate
(but I am September winds.)

Love is nonsensical;
I know that much.

You told me I argue
too much, fight
too much
and I am tired.
(The moon keeps me up
later these days.)

I lie beneath
loosely tucked blankets,
your music festival bracelets
choking me
as I try to sleep.

My sheets reek of eucalyptus
and Jack Daniels
(I taste you in these pillows.)

Tossing about,
I turn towards the moon
(and your window,)
while the planes overhead
rock me
to sleep.

Questions for the Stranger in Front of the Playhouse

Why is it that, as I read, I can see you
in the corner of my eye, like dust,

watching me, your coffee-stained glance
switching to pavement the moment I

look up? Is it this hard-bound beauty
in my fingertips that you wish to hold?

Were you too inclined to pick up
a copy of Whitman's poems,

before nights became days became
nights nestled in lines beneath the eyes

I still feel watching? Or do you look on
the same way I read: lips parted

but not moving, prone to distraction,
constantly fingering the next page?

Sunset Over Sutphin Boulevard

Wreath
hanging on a blue door
of a brick house.

>You,
>your house
>with the blue door,
>sitting where the tracks diverge.

Broken
shutters hiding broken
windows of a being,

>broken
>because being broken
>is not always a choice
>(and sometimes the tracks diverge
>before they ever meet.)

There's something about a sunset
over the tracks
that gets trapped in rusted screens

>and your brick house
>with the blue door
>is something poetic
>for those who ride the trains
>as the tracks diverge
>and never question

why

a wreath hangs

on the blue door

of your brick house

                                                          in April

3a.m. to Coney Island

Your name is cough syrup
for my naivety.

It
goes
down

bitter,

leaving remnants
lingering
hours
on my lips;

but, as my morning tea
slides
down
smooth,

I am thankful

for loose-fitting pullovers
and wind chills.

Saunter at the MoMa

(inspired by the paintings of Philip Gurton and Kazemi Malevich)

I. Short lines, a student pass,
   side-step the coat check
   an escalator takes me
   to the upper floors
   It is early, there are less people,
   I hope.

II. It is Saturday:
    more people

III. I stare inside the wooden frame:
     two buildings, windows--two men smoking
     pipes; one straight
     the other out the corner of his mouth,
     a student
     of film noir.

IV. The bridges are either heart-shaped
    or pornographic.

V. Why is it that I always see
   faces
   in shapes

and inanimate objects?

VI. Interpretation of the question
is half the answer.

VII. Maybe the moon
is where soldiers go
when they die:
bombs exploding, limbs
propelling through space
searching for a landing--
and he is there
smiling, a cradle
for deformities
and nuances, land
of the giant spiders
and bravest of men.

VIII. It is not a gymnast.

It is a face.

IX. Straight lines and rectangles.

X. A plaque to the left reads
suprematism.

XI. It is *abstract.*

XII.   Rectangles
       and straight lines.

       I glance towards a self portrait--
       small head, arms lifting something
       large and red.

XIII. I turn to go
       wondering why
       the books were
       falling
       off the shelves.

Chaos Theory

I swear I saw
moonbeams
shoot out of your fingertips
that night the cosmos
revoked order,

watched stardust flee
from the corners of your smile

lost myself
in the lament
of planetary insomniacs,

as cosmic waves
reverberated,

gravitational paralysis
spiraling us
out of control.

My veins still pulse
from that release
into the arms
of distant galaxies,

the drifting
between infrared disks

detached from orbit

soaring past the pantomime sun,
that traded handstands
for dimes,

while luring
hydrogen
from our lips.

I shut my eyes,
lids heavy
from the day,
as my body rocks
with the tides

into that dark matter
that I know
left us both

trembling
into
combustion.

Lying Backwards in Bed

If to love someone
is to leave them
awake at night
listening to your song
as your scent
teases its way
into their pillow,
I only hope
to never love someone
the way
you
loved
me.

To Friendship

He pulls at the striped collar
fastened in place morning
after morning by patient fingers,
the same ones that brew
a single cup of coffee
for the clay mug
idle by the stove.

Now it rests
on the corner of his desk,
as he watches the world sink
beneath the bay
from the same chair
his father watched from
years before.

A hot Sunday afternoon
crackles in the fireplace
as he takes a sip.

* * *

Miles away, she reads
underneath a cloak of candlelight,
tracing his thin cursive
across the page,
an aroma of honey
and pears

filtering through
the loosened screen
into the night.

She stares at him
through the flame,
watches as he lowers his cup
to the edge of the chipped mahogany,
gaze locked
on his think cursive
as the world
sinks beneath the bay.

on the steps of one's home

one sits,
pen in hand,
notebook open covering knees.

one glances at the berry tree
one used to climb,
one can still taste their sweetness;
one licks one's lips.
(one is forever licking one's berry-stained lips.)

the door to the house looks
smaller than one remembers.
one can feel oneself growing--
(is one growing right now?)
one tugs at one's sleeves.

one places the book on the stairs.
one stands up, starts pacing
(one never could sit still.)

one hums a melody.
one subdivides.
one lifts one's arms and begins conducting
for an audience at the table in front,
party of--

one is lonely.

one pretends one is not lonely;
one closes one's eyes,
conjures an end to lonely.

one's conjurer is broken.

one sits down, picks up the book
and leaves lonely on the page, next to the others
in the same black ink,
always slanted
a bit to the right.

one's hand is tired.

The Seconds Between

We begin by chasing the light,
hoping to end with a bang...

everything else is nothing.

Born from, raised for,
where you and I rest.

The world is small
and we are only a fraction
of a percent of it, place values away
from any point; yet,
we spend evenings toasting the stars,
prayers consumed by the glow.

Nothing.

Here, the pulse of the djembe
wakens our own percussive beat
(we swear it's Sirius in our fingertips.)

Rest assured, though:
when the bang comes,
there is no music.
Pulses cease; Sirius retreats
into the night.

Nothing.

Born from, raised for,
where you and I rest,
somewhere in between the thunder
and the light.

Roadside Memorial

I remember the past
Before there was [death]
I was eight.

I didn't cringe at the sight of lilies,
look upon pillar candles
as a sign of something fallen,
feel death like bacteria on my arms,
hands, palms, neck
that no amount of hot showers
could kill.

My thoughts didn't follow a grim trail from you
to me, repeating itself, again
and again, my footsteps over your last
(those photographs of you--
I associate collages with grief,) again,
footsteps over your last.

My OCD was milder then.

I don't know how it happened,
if it was that bicycle helmet
you refused to wear or your own
slow-moving feet, bad luck with cars,
streets...

Your smile gets caught
in my throat every time I see
a petaled reminder,
a broken flame.

Though your face never stood a chance
in my memory, your lean arms
and white t-shirt blind me
every time another leaves.

purple and orange

I'm going to be
me, you
you

and, if we do not spend nights
talking beneath blankets

or bent by the same words
in the paper, if my dog-whistle

laugh doesn't bring you running,
if it's always purple

never orange or leather
seats instead of bindings,

if no more words
are given
to us

when morning comes
and I flip

through the business
section or watch

the sun set
into violet nights

if you listen
closely
you'll hear

my laugh
in the wind.

Galaxy Surfing on a Knitting Needle

She liked the beat of rain
against dilapidated screens
and fire escapes.
She liked the way patterns made her think.
Her cardigans fit loosely
around her shoulders and her shirts
were always a button off
(she never thought to pull them up.)

She liked Tabasco on everything.
Her dark hair fell to the same side
as her smile.
She wore leg warmers in July
and bit into oranges, sinking
back to the sun.

When she was nine,
she stitched her mouth shut
to hear the night.

"The moon is a fingernail," she said,
and meant it.

She sipped from streams,
toasting roller coasters
and rocket ships.

Her hair thinned
and she stopped bleeding ink
(they didn't notice she took all the words with her.)

She was carried onto the porch by three men
(the rain didn't sound the same.)

Her sleeves were soaked,
legs bare in the hot sun,
eyes closed
as she sank.

Call Me Space Cadet

I. I like to explore the craters of the moon;
    I sleep with the blinds open, bed
    pressed up to the window so,
    at certain angles, on certain nights,
    I can see the crescent as I fall asleep.
    (I think I'd be happier there.)

II. Call me *hippie* because I think war is for the weak
    (and who doesn't enjoy running barefoot,
    blades of grass piercing your skin: man
    and earth, reminders of sandcastles,
    mud pies, swing sets.)

III. Call me *slut* because I think monogamy is why
    marriages don't last, and that divorce lawyers
    are only in it for the pre-settlement sex.

IV. Call me *free spirit*,
    but I am bound by the same flesh encasement
    chastising me every time I step outside the door.

V. Call me *waste of space*--
    I'll get back to you on that one.

VI. Call me *space cadet*. I'm not always
    here; sometimes, I drift.
    I won't pretend I always listen

when people talk, words get lost;
I drift.
I'm not a writer (though I admit
I've called myself *poet* on occasion.)
I write.

If you ask me why, I'll probably tell you
"because it's all I know"
(take that as you wish.)

I write.

I might tell you it's because
it's the only time I'm ever honest
(I do mean that.)

Words tether themselves to the walls
of my mind and, sometimes,
they drift
towards one another,
until there isn't enough space for them without coiling
so I write them into lines,
the only time I'm ever honest.

VII. The other day, I laid beneath my blanket,
your words on repeat like the song you'd played in your car
(I was back there, your hand
folded into mine like origami.)
It wasn't until that night, hands
at either side of the fabric, that your words

strung themselves together, a coil,
bed pressed up to the window,
mind to the moon overhead,
as I reached for the pen.

evening rhythms

again we find ourselves
coerced by the night

ions lost for eons

drifting in
and out
of black holes
and sleep

inside we sit
sobered only by the clarity
in the silence

the only light
comes from
a desk lamp
as we wait

featureless
in its faded glow

figures
projected
onto stained walls

our fingers meet

but never touch

and we remain

silhouettes

Crescendo

This was before the glow sticks
and Yankee Stadium
before the festival of poets
and late-night road trips out of state
and this was certainly before
there was anything other than
you and me.

We were in a baseball field,
throwing pitches,
talking about plane destinations,
and the New York Times.

You, me,
like it had been
so many times before
and yet...

We were in the grass,
arms tiring, tossing pitches,
shifting closer after every one
until we could roll the ball
to each other
within the confines
of the diamond
made from our legs
and feet.

It was dusk
and I let the cold
seep into me
(somehow I knew
you were doing the same.)

Past dusk,
and in quiet agreement
we stood up,
gathered the gloves,
ball,
and headed back
across the grass.

As we neared the gate,
the sprinklers came on
and we forgot the cold,
you,
me,
headfirst into the mist,
heated droplets
dripping from our bodies.

Bookmark

Please keep my place
amongst the pages,
even once my book
has been read.

Tree Rings Discovered Sunspots (and We Will Too)

Think of me as a *work
in progress*, a *to-be-determined*,
a *not-quite-there-yet*.

My hat is neon with *under construction*,
my arms covered in first drafts,
my reflection a question marked in the middle
of a line. I stand out
in ways it would be easier
to sit in as though
my words aren't italicized
in doubt.

I am undeveloped
like the poems that litter
my journal,
(and like the word
freckle I am
scribbled eight times
in the margins.)

A sentence, fragmented
and bleeding red ink.

I am a work in progress,
unannounced, undefined,
indeterminate. I'm not quite there
yet, but the neon doesn't brand me

(I blink color into the pencil
on my eyelids,) my arms
are in revision, and I noticed
that, when I lower
my shoulders,
my outline
looks more
like a comma.

NOTES

"A Pleasure to Burn:" This title comes from the opening line of Ray Bradbury's novel, *Fahrenheit 451*; Simon & Schuster, 2012.

"You're Beautiful:" This poem is based off of Simon Armitage's poem of the same name, from his poetry collection, *The Shout*, Alfred A. Knopf, 2005.

"Descent:" Lines 1-2 are taken from *The Marriage Plot*, by Jeffrey Eugenides; Picador, 2012.

"Roadside Memorial:" Lines 1-3 quote Elizabeth Spires' "Translation of My Life," *The Wave-Maker,* W.W. Norton & Company, 2008.

ACKNOWLEDGEMENTS

Grateful acknowledgment to my editors and friends, Joshua Callahan and Dylan Cahir, without whom I could not have done this.

I wish to thank the Hofstra English Society and its members for providing a community in which I could further explore the writing process.

My gratitude, thanks, and appreciation go to Phillis Levin, Ed Rodriguez, and Vincent Parker for instilling in me an appreciation for words that extends beyond any I could find to describe it, and for cultivating my writing over the years.

Lastly, and with love, to my friends and family for your constant support and feedback, and to my mom, for making all of this possible.

ABOUT THE AUTHOR

Victoria Cocolaras was born and raised in Queens, New York. She earned her Bachelor of Arts degree in creative writing from Hofstra University and currently resides in San Jose, California. When she isn't writing, you can find her wandering amongst the many bookshelves at Books Inc. in Mountain View, California. This is her first collection of poetry.

CPSIA information can be obtained
at www.ICGtesting.com
Printed in the USA
FSHW011251181019
63165FS